First World War
and Army of Occupation
War Diary
France, Belgium and Germany

2 DIVISION
2 Light Brigade
London Regiment
9th (County of London) Battalion (Queen Victoria's Rifles)
1 March 1919 - 24 October 1919

WO95/1374/7

The Naval & Military Press Ltd
www.nmarchive.com
Published in association with The National Archives

Published by

The Naval & Military Press Ltd

Unit 10 Ridgewood Industrial Park,

Uckfield, East Sussex,

TN22 5QE England

Tel: +44 (0) 1825 749494

www.naval-military-press.com

www.nmarchive.com

This diary has been reprinted in facsimile from the original. Any imperfections are inevitably reproduced and the quality may fall short of modern type and cartographic standards.

© **Crown Copyright**
Images reproduced by permission of The National Archives, London, England, 2015.

Contents

Document type	Place/Title	Date From	Date To
Heading	WO95/1374/7		
Heading	2 Division 2 Light Brigade 9 London Regt 1919 March-1919 Oct From 58 Div 175 Bde		
War Diary	Duren	01/03/1919	13/04/1919
War Diary	Niederaussem	14/04/1919	30/04/1919
War Diary	Niederaussem Oberaussem	01/05/1919	31/05/1919
Miscellaneous	Warning Order	23/05/1919	23/05/1919
Miscellaneous	Appendix II		
Miscellaneous	2nd Light Brigade Special Order	17/05/1919	17/05/1919
War Diary	Niederaussem Oberaussem	01/06/1919	25/06/1919
War Diary	Riehl Barracks Cologne	26/06/1919	30/06/1919
Miscellaneous	Appendix I	16/06/1919	16/06/1919
Miscellaneous	Appendix II	17/06/1919	17/06/1919
Miscellaneous	Relief Of Guards Found By 1st Northern Brigade Cologne Area	16/06/1919	16/06/1919
Miscellaneous	Orders For The Battalion Move To The Niederaussem Area	02/07/1919	02/07/1919
War Diary	Niederaussem & Oberaussem	01/07/1919	01/07/1919
War Diary	Germany 1/25000 3a Sheet S.W	02/07/1919	09/07/1919
War Diary	Wald Germany 1/25000 25 SW & NW	10/07/1919	31/07/1919
Miscellaneous	Orders For Move To Lowland Divisional Area		
Miscellaneous	Move To Lowland Division Area	08/07/1919	08/07/1919
Miscellaneous	Outpost Sector Held by 9th London Regiment		
War Diary	Wald Germany 1/25000 25 SW & NW	01/08/1919	15/08/1919
War Diary	Wald	16/08/1919	31/08/1919
Miscellaneous	Headquarters 2nd Light Brigade		
War Diary	Wald	01/10/1919	24/10/1919

woods|13|14|7 2|14|14|7

2. ~~E~~ DIVISION

2. LIGHT BRIGADE

9 LONDON REGT

1919 MARCH — 1919 OCT

FROM 58 DIV 175 BDE

Army Form C. 2118.

9th London Regt / Queen Victorias Rifles

WAR DIARY
or
INTELLIGENCE SUMMARY.
(Erase heading not required.)

Place	Date	Hour	Summary of Events and Information	Remarks and references to Appendices
DÜREN	1919 March 1		Day spent in train travelling from HERVE (BELGIUM) to DÜREN (GERMANY)	
	2	9h00	Detrained at DÜREN marched to billets in that town. "A" "B" Coys billeted in the school	
			PHILIP STRASSE "C" + "D" Coys in the theatre STADT PARK	
	3rd	11 hrs	C.O's Parade	Wet afternoon
	4th	9.30h	Batln Parade, Route March	Games Co
	5th	9.30h	Commanding Officers Parade	Recreational
	6th		Coys at the disposal of O's.C. Coys. Baths during day for all Coys	Training etc
	7th	9.30h	Batln Parade Route March	
	8th		Coys at the disposal of O's.C. Coys. Boden Disinfector for use of A+B Coys. R.E. working party 1 Offr 300R	
	9th	9.30h	Church Parade	
	10th		Coys at the disposal of O's.C. Coys for training. N.C.Os class commenced.	
	11th	9.30h	Commanding Officers Parade. N.C.O's Hotax Lunches	
	12th		Coys at disposal of O's C Coys for training on Musketry Lewis Gun Specialist classes as above	
	13th		" " " Baths for the Batln. Specialist classes held	
	14th		Batln Route March	"
	15th	9.30h	Commanding Officers Parade. M.O's inspection for all Coys. Baths for details	

M.C. Lt Col
Commanding 9th Batln London Regt

Army Form C. 2118.

WAR DIARY
or
INTELLIGENCE SUMMARY.

9th Battn Queens Victorias Rifles

(Erase heading not required.)

Instructions regarding War Diaries and Intelligence Summaries are contained in F. S. Regs., Part II. and the Staff Manual respectively. Title pages will be prepared in manuscript.

Place	Date	Hour	Summary of Events and Information	Remarks and references to Appendices
DÜREN	1919 MARCH 16th	11 am	Church Parade at the Garrison Church	
	17th	9.30 am	Commanding Officers Parade. Specialist classes held for NCOs, Lewis Gunners, Signals, S.Bs.	
	18th		Coys at disposal of O's C Coys	
	19th	9.30 am	Commanding Officers Parade "	
	20th		Coys at disposal of O's C Coys. 10 Offrs + 5 ORs sent for demobilisation	
	21st	9.30 am	Baths. Route March. Specialist classes held (as above)	
	22nd		Coys at disposal of O's C Coys. Medical inspection of Battn. Specialist classes	
	23rd	9.30 am	Church Parade in the Y.M.C.A.	
	24th		Coys at disposal of O's C Coys. Specialist classes (as above)	
	25th		" "	
	26th	9.30 am	Commanding Officers Parade	
	27th		Coys at disposal of O's C Coys. Baths for Battn. The R.A. String band visits DÜREN	
	28th		" " " "A" Coy ordered to "stand by" in billets - trouble expected.	
			By strikers of neighbouring village - nothing happened.	
	29th		Coys at disposal of O's C Coys. Medical inspection of the Battn. Baths for Battn.	
		2.0 pm	1 Officer + 10 ORs sent for demobilisation	

J.W. Boult Lt. Col.
Commanding 9th Battn Queens Rifles.

Army Form C. 2118.

WAR DIARY
9th Batt London Regt or Queen Victoria Rifles
INTELLIGENCE SUMMARY.
(Erase heading not required.)

Instructions regarding War Diaries and Intelligence Summaries are contained in F. S. Regs., Part II. and the Staff Manual respectively. Title pages will be prepared in manuscript.

Place	Date	Hour	Summary of Events and Information	Remarks and references to Appendices
DUREN.	1919 March 30	11 am	Church Parade in NBA	
	31st		Coys at disposal of O's C Coys. Specialist Courses held.	

Lieut Col.
Commanding 9th Batt London Regt

WAR DIARY or Intelligence Summary

9th Infantry / Queen Victoria's Rifles

Army Form C. 2118.

Place	Date	Hour	Summary of Events and Information	Remarks and references to Appendices
DÜREN	4/9 17/8/21	9.30	Batt. parade drills. Specialist classes. N.C.Os. Signals & Stretcher Bearers	Map of Germany 1/5
	2		10.0pm 300 Oks. arrived from 2nd Q.V.R.s. Coy at disposal of O.s C. Coy Specialist classes	
	3		Coy at disposal of Coy Commdrs. Coy to Coy 3.0pm 400 Oks. left for attachment to the ROYAL DRAGOONS PAFFENDORF	
	4		Coy at disposal of Coy Commdrs for training. 6.0 inspected K.R.R.C draft Specialist classes Route March	
	5		" " " " " Weapon inspection of all Coys Route March	
	6	11	Church Parade in Y.M.C.A. Warning order for move following day	
	7	12.45	Am moved from DÜREN entraining at DÜREN station 12.45 hours. Detrained at ROMMERSKIRCHEN and marched to billets A.B. Coys "HQ" NIEDERAUSSEM 'C' & 'D' Coys OBERAUSSEM	Germany 1/2 M1
	8		Coys at disposal of O.s C. Coys for cleaning up & settling into billets	
	9		" " " Baths at Portuna factory for C & D Coys	
	10		" " " A.B. HQ Coys	
	11	9.30-2.30	" " " for training	
	12	9.30	C.Os Parade Lieut Col R.B Powell D.S.O. Rifle Bde assumed command of the Bn vice Lieut Col G.R. Powell Grenadier Guards	
	13	9.30	Church Parade in Y.M.C.A. NIEDERAUSSEM	R.B. Powell Lieut Col Commanding 9th Bn. Lon. Regiment.

Army Form C. 2118.

WAR DIARY
or Intelligence Summary

9th Bn London Regt (Queen Victorias Rifles)

(Erase heading not required.)

Place	Date	Hour	Summary of Events and Information	Remarks and references to Appendices
NIEDERAUSSEM	1919 April 14	9 to 13hr	Coy training under O.C. Coy. Educational classes for all men who cannot read from the Army 3rd class certificates 12 – 15 hours	
	15	9.15	Maker/route March	
	16	9-13hrs	Coy training under O.C. Coy Educational classes as above	
	17	"	" " " " Football 14-30hrs C v D Coys	
	18	10	Voluntary Church Service YMCA Educational classes as above	
	19	9-13hrs	Coy training under O.C. Coy Football 14-30hrs Officers v Sgts	
	20	10	Church Parade YMCA NIEDERAUSSEM. Football 14-30hrs Sr. v 4/5 Pla Coy R.E.	
	21		No Parades Coy Sports during the day	
	22	9-13hrs	Coy training under O.C. Coy Baths Educational classes as above	
	23	9.15	Batt'n route March including 1st Line Transport.	
	24		Batt'n inspected by Brig Gen R A Curran CMG DSO Commanding 2nd Reg'd Inf Bde. Educational as above	
	25		" " Maj Gen Sir R D Whigham KCB DSO Commanding Light Division	
	26		Coy training under O.C. Coy Billet inspection by Commanding Officer	
	27	9.30	Church Parade YMCA NIEDERAUSSEM.	

R Parrot Lieut Col
Commanding 9th Bn London v Regt.

Army Form C. 2118.

WAR DIARY
or ~~Intelligence~~ SUMMARY.

9th London Regt / Queen Victoria Rifles

(Erase heading not required.)

Instructions regarding War Diaries and Intelligence Summaries are contained in F. S. Regs., Part II. and the Staff Manual respectively. Title pages will be prepared in manuscript.

Place	Date	Hour	Summary of Events and Information	Remarks and references to Appendices
NIEDERPUSSEN	28th	9.30 a.m.	Coy training under O.C. Coys. Specialist classes for Lewis Gun, L.Ms, Signallers & for N.C.Os Education	
	29th	"	"	
	30th	9.15	Bath. Route March	

J.P. Black
Lieut Colonel
Commanding 9th London Regt

(A7883) D. J. & L., London, E.C. Wt. W807/M1672 350,000 4/17 Sch. 52a Forms/C/2118/14

Army Form C. 2118.

WAR DIARY or INTELLIGENCE SUMMARY.

Queen Victorias Rifles 9th London Regt.

(Erase heading not required.)

Place	Date	Hour	Summary of Events and Information	Remarks and references to Appendices
NIEDERAUSSEM	MAY 1.		Platoon Training	GERMANY 1st M.I.
OBERAUSSEM	2.		" "	
	3.		" "	
	4.		Church Parade	
	5.		Platoon Training. Major C.F. ROTHSCHILD DSO. M.C. to command for two L. Cos. E.B. POWELL DSO to ARMY.	
	6.		" "	
	7.		" "	
	8.		" "	
	9.		" "	
	10.		" "	
	11.		Church Parade	
	12.		Platoon Training	
	13.		" "	
	14.		" "	
	15.		" "	
	16.		Bn. inspected by Brigadier Gen. R.M. CURRIE CMG DSO commanding 2nd Light Brigade	

F.R. Day Lieut: Colonel,
O.C. Queen Victorias Rifles.

Army Form C. 2118.

9th London Regt "Queen Victorias Rifles"

WAR DIARY or INTELLIGENCE SUMMARY.

(Erase heading not required.)

Instructions regarding War Diaries and Intelligence Summaries are contained in F. S. Regs., Part II. and the Staff Manual respectively. Title pages will be prepared in manuscript.

Place	Date	Hour	Summary of Events and Information	Remarks and references to Appendices
NIEDERAUSSEM	17		2nd Light Brigade inspected by General Sir William R. Robertson GCB KCVO DSO ADC Commander-in-Chief British Army of the Rhine. Complimentary letter received on parade.	GERMANY 1917 M.1. Appendix III
OBERAUSSEM	18		Wednesday Church Parade	
	19		Battn training	
	20		" "	
	21		" "	
	22		" "	
	23		Lt. Col. J.R. Day, Norfolk Regt to command Bn.	
			"Warning order received that Battn to be prepared to move forward"	
			AREA in event of trouble, our peace terms the Army having to move forward. Orders issued to Coy as per Appendix I. And a list of guides to be found on for	
	24		Appendix II	
	25		Battn training	
	26		Church Parade	
	27		Battn training	
	28		" "	

J.R. Day, Lieut. Colonel.
O.C. Queen Victorias Rifles.

Army Form C. 2118.

WAR DIARY
or
INTELLIGENCE SUMMARY.

9th London Regt Queen Victoria Rifles

(Erase heading not required.)

Instructions regarding War Diaries and Intelligence Summaries are contained in F. S. Regs., Part II. and the Staff Manual respectively. Title pages will be prepared in manuscript.

Place	Date	Hour	Summary of Events and Information	Remarks and references to Appendices
NEIDERAUSSEM /OBERAUSSEM	29		Platoon training	
	30		" "	
	31		" "	

J.R.D. Lieut Colonel
O.C. Queen Victorias Rifles

APPENDIX I

SECRET.

WARNING ORDER.

"C" and "D" Companies will be prepared to move to the Cologne Area tomorrow the 24th at short notice.

Dress: Fighting Order.   Packs will be carried by lorry.

If baggage wagons are not provided for Company Stores each Company will detail a guard of one N.C.O. and six Men to remain behind.   Area Stores such as Beds, Latrine Buckets, etc., will not be taken.   Battle Limbers, Cookers and Pack Mules will accompany their respective Companies.

Detailed orders will be issued later.

Signed.   R. O. BETTS.
Captain & Adjutant,
Queen Victoria's Rifles.

23rd May, 1919.

TO:- All Coys   APPENDIX II

In order to make the necessary preparations for a move to the Cologne Area the undermentioned instructions are issued to enable O.C. Companies to warn the N.C.O.s and Men for the various guards.

O.C. "A" Company will find the following guards:-

No. 2 Post, Detention Barracks, consisting of 2 N.C.O.s and 8 Other Ranks.

No. 5 Post, Bon Tor Station, consisting of 2 N.C.O.s and 8 Other Ranks.

No. 7 Post, C.-in-C's House, consisting of 2 N.C.O.s and 14 Other Ranks.

No. 4 Post, Fort Seven, consisting of 2 Officers, 3 N.C.O.s and 21 Other Ranks, including 2 Signallers and 2 Lewis Guns.   Men on this post have to learn the German Machine Gun with which the Fort is defended.

No.11 Post, The Militare Lazarette, Kartaussen Wall, Ordnance Depot, consisting of 1 N.C.O. and 6 Other Ranks.

No. 9 Post, Vehicle Guard, consisting of 2 N.C.O.s and 8 Other Ranks.

Total: 2 Officers, 12 N.C.O.s, 65 O.R.s

Company Headquarters will be at the Artillery Barracks, in the Bonner Strasse.

O.C. "B" Company will find the following guards:-

No. 8 Post, Eiffel Tor Station, consisting of 1 Officer, 4 N.C.O.s and 41 Other Ranks.

No.10 Post, No.44 C.C.S, at Umbringen, consisting of 2 N.C.O.s and 10 Other Ranks.

No.12 Post, E.F.C. Depot, at Bayern Strasse, consisting of 1 N.C.O. and 6 Men.
Total: 1 Officer, 7 N.C.O.s, 57 Other Ranks.

Company Headquarters as for "A" Company.

APPENDIX 11

O.C. "C" Company will find the following guards:-

No. 3 Post, The Powder Magazine, Radenburd, consisting of
4 Officers, 10 N.C.O.s and 70 Other Ranks.

Company Headquarters, the Powder Magazine.

O.C. "D" Company will find the following guards:-

No. 1 Post, The Docks, Marienburg, consisting of 3 Officers,
12 N.C.O.s and 73 Men.

No. 6 Post, Train Guard, consisting of 3 N.C.O.s and
24 Other Ranks.

Total: 3 Officers, 15 N.C.O.s and 97 O.R.s

"D" Company Headquarters, The Docks.

O.C. Companies can see a Map at the Battalion Orderly Room showing where all these posts are.
In view of a move being ordered troops will move by lorry, and each Company will take its Lewis Guns and eight drums per gun with them.

Captain and Adjutant,
Queen Victoria's Rifles.

APPENDIX III

2nd LIGHT BRIGADE.

SPECIAL ORDER.

The Commander-in-Chief has requested me to express to every Officer, N.C.O and man of the 2nd Light Brigade his personal appreciation of the soldierlike manner in which to-day's parade for his inspection was carried out.

He was very favourably impressed by the smartness and turnout of all ranks, by their steadiness on parade, and by the precision with which both the troops and the transport marched past him.

The result reflects great credit on all concerned, and I look to each Battalion in the Brigade to do its utmost, not only to maintain but to improve upon, the reputation it has gained to-day.

The 2nd Light Brigade has not long been formed, but it has started well. I feel confident that all ranks, by their soldierly bearing both on and off parade, by the zeal and energy with which they enter into their training and their games, and by a high sense of esprit de corps and good comradeship, will in the future aim at producing a higher standard of all round military efficiency than can be found in any other formation of the British Army of the Rhine.

Brigadier General,
Commanding 2nd Light Brigade.

May 17th, 1919.

Army Form C. 2118.

WAR DIARY
or
INTELLIGENCE SUMMARY.
(Erase heading not required.)

9th London Regt. or Queen Victoria's Rifles

Place	Date	Hour	Summary of Events and Information	Remarks and references to Appendices
NIEDERAUSSEM +OBERAUSSEM	JUNE 1st	10.15	Church Parade	Map of GERMANY 1/25000 Sheet 32 S.W.
	2nd		Batt. Training	
	3	10	Ceremonial Parade in celebration of His Majesty's birthday. Remainder of day observed as holiday	
	4		Company Training	
	5		Batt. Training	
	6		" "	
	7		Batt. Interior Economy & Company Training	
	8	10.15	Church Parade	
	9		Whitsun Bank Holiday	
	10		Company "	
	11		Batt. Training	
	12		" "	
	13		" "	
	14		The Officer Commanding IV Corps inspected Bill'ts cookhouses etc of the battn. Training	
	15	10.15	Church Parade. Warning order received that "I" day would probably be Friday June 20th. I-3 Tuesday 17.	17-3 the day prior to commencement of an actual mobile warfare.

Instructions to Coy Commanders as per Appendix I

J.R. Bay
Lieut: Colonel,
O.C. Queen Victoria's Rifles.

Army Form C. 2118.

WAR DIARY or INTELLIGENCE SUMMARY.

9th London Regt or Queen Victorias Rifle.

(Erase heading not required.)

Instructions regarding War Diaries and Intelligence Summaries are contained in F.S. Regs., Part II. and the Staff Manual respectively. Title pages will be prepared in manuscript.

Place	Date	Hour	Summary of Events and Information	Remarks and references to Appendices
NIEDERAUSSEM	16		Company Battn Training	
OBERAUSSEM	17	0900	Order received that J-3 day would be today. Orders issued (vide Appendix II) to act on instructions issued (APPENDIX III) four Companies entrained at Quadrath for MARIENBURG BARRACKS COLOGNE. Headquarters remained at NIEDERAUSSEM	
	18		Four Companies remained by 1st NORTHERN BRIGADE (as per Army for May) Battn. H.Q. moved by road to the School PLATZEN STRASSE BICKENDORF	
	19		Bn. H.Q. moves by road to RIEHL BARRACKS COLOGNE. Vacated by 51st D.L.I.	
	20		Battn remained in same locations	
	21		"	
	22		18th Bn K.R.R.C. relieves part of the Guards found by the Battn 12th The Docks guard (2) The Powder magazine (3) The Combs guard. Two whole Companies (C+D) being relieved. On relief they marches to RIEHL BARRACKS, joins H.Q.	
	23		C and D Companies in RIEHL BARRACKS - Company training A and B Companies on Guard duties in Cologne.	
	24		ditto	
	25		ditto	

F.R. Day. Lieut Colonel
O.C. Queen Victorias Rifles

Army Form C. 2118.

WAR DIARY
or
INTELLIGENCE SUMMARY.

9th Battn. London Regt. Queen Victoria Rifles.

(Erase heading not required.)

Place	Date	Hour	Summary of Events and Information	Remarks and references to Appendices
RIEHL BARRACKS COLOGNE.	26		"C" and "D" Companies in RIEHL BARRACKS — Company training. "A" and "B" Companies on guard duties in Cologne.	
	27		ditto	
	28		ditto. Orders received that	
	29		"A" day with Reps Ministry 30.6.19. "C" and "D" Companies. Church Parade. "A" and "B" Companies Guardsdutio. Instructions issued to Companies as per Appendix 14, giving details as to moving back to NIEDERAUSSEM Area on July 1st 1919.	
	30		"C" and "D" Companies' training. "A" and "B" Companies march to RIEHL BARRACKS after being relieved of their guard duties by the 51st NORTHUMBERLAND FUSLRS. Small advanced party sent to NIEDERAUSSEM to arrange billets etc.	

R. Day.
Lieut: Colonel,
O.C. Queen Victoria Rifles.

C O P Y   APPENDIX I   S E C R E T.
*********   ***********

To/
Capt. R.S. Johnson,
Lieut A.G. Croll, M.C.
Capt. H. d'Argenton.
Capt. W. Gray, M.C.

A Warning Order has been received that Guards in COLOGNE may have to be taken over by this Battalion tomorrow. This will be confirmed later.

No orders will be issued, and no one in your Company is to be told.

You will proceed to COLOGNE this afternoon on the 1331 train from ROMMERSKIRCHEN to inspect all posts that are to be found by your Company in accordance with instructions previously issued.

(Signed)   R.O. BETTS,
Captain & Adjutant,
Queen Victoria's Rifles.

16/6/1919.

ROB 2.
======

C O P Y
****

APPENDIX II

SECRET.
========

To

    J-3 day, today, Tuesday 17th June. Act on instructions as issued under my R.O.B. 1. Acknowledge.

                  (Signed) R.O. BETTS,
                            Captain and Adjutant,
                            Queen Victoria's Rifles.

17/6/1919.

C O P Y   APPENDIX III

ROB 1.   SECRET.

RELIEF OF GUARDS FOUND BY 1st NORTHERN BRIGADE, COLOGNE AREA.

1. In the event of orders being received to take over guards at present being found by the 1st Northern Brigade, the Battalion will move as follows:-

   J-3 day, 4 companies to Artillery Barracks, MARIENBURG.

   J-2 day, 4 companies to relieve guards in accordance with instructions issued.

   J-2 day, Battalion Headquarters move into School at SUBELRATER, BICKENDORF.

   J-1 day, Battalion Headquarters move RIEHL Barracks.

   J-2 day, 4 companies to be relieved by 1st Light Brigade and will join Battalion Headquarters at RIEHL Barracks.

2. On J-3 day, lorries as shewn below will report to each Company Headquarters at 0900 hours.

              "A" Company ... ... 5 lorries
              "B" Company ... ... 5 lorries
              "C" Company ... ... 5 lorries
              "D" Company ... ... 5 lorries

   In addition 3 lorries will be allotted to Battalion Headquarters for J-2 and J-1 days. All troops moving by lorry will proceed in full marching order, those moving by road will move in battle order and packs will be taken on lorries. Companies will as far as possible take all Company Stores with the exception of barrack furniture, ablution benches, latrine seats, etc., which will be dumped, in the case of "A" and "B" Companies at the Q.M. Stores, and "C" and "D" Companies at "D" Company's Guard Room.
        O.C. "H.Q" will detail an Guard consisting of 1 N.C.O. and 6 O.R.s from the Regimental Police to remain behind for the dump in NIEDERAUSSEM, and O.C. "C" Company a Guard of the same strength for the dump in OBERAUSSEM. O.C. Companies will be held responsible that all Government property is collected and dumped. Billets and Dining Halls vacated will be left clean and tidy

3. **SUPPLIES.** Refilling will be as under:-

   J-3 day, refilling at RHEIDT as usual.

   J-2 day, no refilling

   J-1 day, RIEHL Barracks, 1100 hours.

   J day and onwards, RIEHL Barracks at normal time.

   On J-3 day, companies will move with rations for the day on the man, and rations for J-2 day in bulk on the lorry. Rations for J-1 day will be sent from Headquarters direct to MARIENBURG Barracks on J-3 day; this wagon will remain at MARIENBURG Barracks on night of J-3/J-2 and report at No.2 Company Train at RIEHL Barracks on afternoon of J-2 day.

4. TRANSPORT.
Company Cookers, Battle Limbers and Pack Animals will proceed on J-3 day to Artillery Barracks, MARIENBURG, by march route under the orders of Second Lieut H.T. WHITTAKER.
One lorry allotted to "A" and "B" Companies will be used to take Company Stores, Officers' Kits and rations in bulk for J-2 day, and ¾ lorry of "C" and "D" Companies will be used for the same purpose.

5. The following amendments have been made to Guards:-

EIFFELTOR Goods Station .... 1 Officer, 5 N.C.O.s 40 O.R.s.

Commander-in-Chief's House .... 2 N.C.O.s, 15 O.R.s.

6. LEWIS GUNS.
On J-3 day Companies moving will take their Lewis Guns and 8 drums per gun with them on the lorry.

7. Acknowledge receipt of these instructions.

(Signed) R. O. BETTS,
Captain & Adjutant,
Queen Victoria's Rifles.

16/6/1919.

ROB 9.   *Appendix IV*   SECRET.

ORDERS FOR THE BATTALION MOVE TO THE NIEDERAUSSEM AREA

ON TUESDAY, 1st JULY, 1919.

1. **MOVE.** The Battalion will proceed by 'bus to the NIEDERAUSSEM Area on Tuesday, 1sy July. Companies will take over all their old billets.

2. **PARADE.** Companies will parade on the Barrack Square at 0845 hours and will be told off into embussing parties 20 strong for embussing. 'Buses are allotted to Companies as under. Lieut A.L. GRACIE, MC. is detailed as Embussing Officer and will see that the Store Buses are sent to the Company Orderly Rooms to collect Company Stores. O.C. "H.Q" Company will detail 2 Runners to report to this Officer at 0845 hours.

"HQ" Company	...	8 Personnel & Stores.		
"A" "	...	5 "	1	Stores.
"B" "	...	4 "	1	"
"C" "	...	5 "	1	"
"D" "	...	4 "	1	"

    Company Lewis Guns, 8 drums per Gun and blankets for the men will be carried on the busses with the men.
    DRESS:- Marching Order, soft caps will be worn.

3. **TRANSPORT.** The Transport will proceed by march route under the orders of Sec. Lieut H.T. WHITTAKER. Cookers will prepare the mid-day meal on the line of march. The Transport will be ready to move off at 0700 hours. All limbers will be loaded over-night. Distances will be maintained in accordance with G.H.Q. Pamphlet on "March Discipline".

4. **REAR PARTY.** O.C. "D" Company will detail a rear party of 1 Officer and 20 Other Ranks to clean up the Barracks. This Officer will obtain a receipt from the in-coming unit that the Barracks have been left in a satisfactory condition. 'Bus for this party will report at the Barracks at 1400 hours.

5. **LOADING PARTY.** Party as dstailed above will report to the Q.M. Stores at 0600 hours for loading purposes.

6. **BARRACKS.** O.C. Companies will render a certificate to the Adjutant at 0830 hours that all Barrack rooms, dining rooms, latrines, etc., have been left clean and tidy. The Messing Officer will render a similar certificate for the Officers' Mess and Men's Cookhouses.

7. **STORES.** 5 Lorries will report to the Q.M. Stores at 0500 hours and 1 Bus at 1400 hours. All stores will be dumped at the Q.M. Stores on Monday night. Officers' Valises and Mess Utensils, etc., will be dumped by 0800 hours.

8. **SUPPLIES.** Refilling on Monday 30th June will be as follows:-

    As usual at 0900 hours and again at 1400 hours.

    Rations for Tuesday will be carried on the Company Cookers and on the Men. Rations for Wednesday will be carried on the supply wagons which will accompany the Transport. After delivering these rations to the Q.M. Stores at NIEDERAUSSEM the wagons will rejoin their Company at RHEIDT.

9. **STATES.** Company Embussing States in duplicate will be rendered to the E.O.R. by 0800 hours.

10. **ACKNOWLEDGE.**

H.Q. 2nd Light Bde.

Forwarded copy of War Diary for July 1919

S. Crall Lt.
fr Lieut: Colonel,
O.C. Queen Victoria's Rifles.

WAR DIARY or **INTELLIGENCE SUMMARY**

Army Form C. 2118.

9th Battn. London Regt. Queen Victoria's Rifles.

Place	Date	Hour	Summary of Events and Information	Remarks and references to Appendices
NIEDERAUSSEM Germany 1/25000 3A Sheet S.W.	JULY 1	0900	Battn. Returned from RIEHL BARRACKS (COLOGNE) to NIEDERAUSSEM & OBERAUSSEM in motor lorries.	
	2		Companies cleaning up billets.	
	3		Company training.	
	4		ditto.	
			Warning orders received that Light Division moves to Lowland Divisional area around SOLINGEN probably on July 8th by rail.	
	5		Company training. B Coy on miniature range at NIEDERAUSSEM. Message received from Brigade that the move will be postponed until the 9th July.	
	6		Church parade at OBERAUSSEM. Thanksgiving Service.	
	7		Preparing to move. Orders issued to Companies, as per Appendix I, with reference to the move to WALD area.	
	8		Preparation for move. Advance party leaves NIEDERAUSSEM in motor lorries and proceeds to WALD to take over Billets and Stores etc. from the 6th Battn. K.O.S.B. D Coy and two platoons* C Coy moved in lorries into the area outside in relief of 6th Battn. K.O.S.B. as per Appendix I.	*for outpost sector see Appendix II
	9		Battn. moves to WALD as per instructions received Companies on the 8th (Appendix I). C Coy - less two platoons move up to outposts to join the two platoons which moved up on the 8. 7.19.	

J R Day Lt Col
CAPT. & ADJUTANT
9 BATTN. LONDON REGT
(QUEEN VICTORIA'S RIFLES.)

Army Form C. 2118.

WAR DIARY
or INTELLIGENCE SUMMARY.
(Erase heading not required.)

9th London Regt Queen Victorias Rifles

Instructions regarding War Diaries and Intelligence Summaries are contained in F. S. Regs., Part II. and the Staff Manual respectively. Title pages will be prepared in manuscript.

Place	Date	Hour	Summary of Events and Information	Remarks and references to Appendices
WAID	July 10		Bn (less C&D Coys) on outpost line) clearing up & settling into billets	
Germany 1/5000 2s. Sh. 11M.	11		"B" Coy duties "A" Coy training - C&D Coys outpost line	
	12		" " " "	
	13		Church Parade	
	14		"B" Coy duties "A" Coy training C&D Coys outpost line	
	15		" " " "	
	16		" " " "	
	17		" " " "	
	18		" " " "	
	19		General Holiday	
	20		Church Parade	
	21		"B" Coy duties "A" Coy training C&D Coys outpost line	
	22		" " " "	
	23		General Holiday	
	24		"B" Coy duties "A" Coy	
	25		" " "	

J R Day
Lieut: Colonel,
O.C. Queen Victorias Rifles.

Army Form C. 2118.

WAR DIARY
or
INTELLIGENCE SUMMARY

Queen Victorias Rifles. 9th London Regt.

(Erase heading not required.)

Instructions regarding War Diaries and Intelligence Summaries are contained in F.S. Regs., Part II. and the Staff Manual respectively. Title pages will be prepared in manuscript.

Place	Date	Hour	Summary of Events and Information	Remarks and references to Appendices
WARD. Germany 1/25000 2s Sheets S, M, N, M	July 26		"B" Coy duties; "A" Coy relieved "C" Coy in the left sector of the outpost line	
	27		"C" Coy moving into WARD occupied by "A" Coy. "B" Coy relieves "D" Coy on outpost line	
	28		Church Parade. "C" Coy took over duties from "B" Coy. "A" on outpost line	
	29		"C" Coy duties. "B" Coy on day training "A" on outpost line	
	30		" " "	
	31		Brigade (less "A" & part of "C" Coy) Route March	

J R Dill
Lieut: Colonel,
O.C. Queen Victorias Rifles.

R.O.B.11.   *Appendix I*   Sheet 1

SECRET.

ORDERS FOR MOVE TO LOWLAND DIVISIONAL AREA.

Ref. Map 2.K. 100,000.

1. **MOVE.** The Battalion will move to the Lowland Divisional Area on July 9th, and will relieve the 6th Battalion K.O.S.B. in the WALD Area.

2. **DRESS.** Marching Order all ranks. Soft Caps and S.B.R.s will be worn.

3. **ADVANCE COMPANIES.** "D" Company and two platoons of "C" Company will proceed by lorries on Tuesday, June the 8th at 1500 hours, to relieve the posts on the frontier at present being found by the 6th K.O.S.B. The following posts will be taken over.

    No.1 Post, KLUSE: 5 N.C.O.s and 25 O.R.s
    No.2 Post, HOHE: 2 N.C.O.s and 9 O.R.s
    No.3 Post, LOOP: 2 N.C.O.s and 17 O.R.s

    The platoon and section organization will be maintained in taking over all guards. All defence schemes, facilities for training, regulations and orders as to frontier posts and area stores will be taken over. Lewis Guns complete and 8 drums per gun will be taken on the lorry. The unexpended portion and one extra day's ration will be taken.

4. **ADVANCE PARTY.** Separate instructions issued. A lorry for this party will report at Battalion Headquarters at 0600 hours on Tuesday.

5. **ENTRAINMENT.** The Battalion will entrain at ROMMERSKIRCHEN. Time to be notified later. 2/Lieut KING is detailed as entraining Officer. Entraining stated will be submitted at 0700 hours on the morning of the move.

6. **LOADING PARTY.** "A" Company will detail one platoon as loading party. This party will load up the lorries at the Q.M. Stores and will proceed to the station on lorries, loading stores on to the train. This party will also do the off-loading at OHLIGS, and will remain until all stores are cleared from the station. This party will be in charge of all baggage and stores after leaving the Q.M. Stores.

7. **TRANSPORT.** Only the undermentioned transport will entrain with the Unit:

    Riders
    7 Limbers
    5 Cookers
    1 Water Cart
    4 G.S. Wagons.

    The remaining transport will proceed by march route under the orders of the Transport Officer. Separate orders will be issued re route and staging, &c.

8. **STORES.** (a) All Barrack and area stores will be handed over to the in-coming unit (e.g: beds, paillasses, tents, latrines buckets, meat safes, ablution benches, soyer stoves, &c.). Receipts will be obtained in duplicate and one copy sent to the B.O.R. The same procedure will be carried out at the other end. These stores will be collected into Company Stores before handing over.

Sheet II

8. <u>STORES</u>. (b) Blankets (rolled in bundles of ten and properly labelled) will be stacked at Company Stores at a time to be notified later. The second suit should be labelled and packed into paillasses by platoons. Times of all stores, officers' kits, &c., will be notified later.

9. <u>BILLETS</u>. Certificates of cleanliness of all billets will be obtained by O.C. Companies signed by an Officer of the relieving unit and sent to the B.O.R.

10. <u>DEFENCE SCHEMES</u>. All defence schemes will be handed over.

11. <u>SUPPLIES</u>. There will be a double refilling on the 8th. The first refilling will be done by 1st Line Transport, and the second by Supply Wagons, the latter remaining with the unit until the completion of the move.
    The unexpended portion of the day's ration for the 9th will be carried on the man.

12. <u>COMPLETION OF RELIEF</u>. The completion of relief by companies will be sent to the B.O.R. at 198 Kaiser Strasse, WALD.

    <u>ACKNOWLEDGE</u>.

                                  (Signed)   R.O. BETTS,
                                                Captain & Adjutant,
                                          Queen Victoria's Rifles.

SECRET.

MOVE TO LOWLAND DIVISION AREA. *Appendix II*

With reference to R.O.B.11.

Para. 5.   The Battalion will entrain at ROMMERSKIRCHEN at 0800 hours. Major H.G.R. BURGES-SHORT, DSO., and the Unit Entraining Officer will report to the R.T.O. at 0720 hours. The Battalion will parade at 0615 hours in Column of Route. Order of march, Headquarters, "A","B" and "C" Companies (less two platoons); head of column at the Junction of MARE STREET and HIGH STREET, NIEDERAUSSEM.

Para. 6.   The loading party (2 platoons of "A" Company) will report to the Quartermaster's Stores at 0700 hours. Train for baggage will be ready for loading at 1000 hours. Quartermaster's Stores will leave one N.C.O. and 5 O.R.s to proceed with the train; and "C" Company one N.C.O. and 3 men to load Company stores at OBERAUSSEM.

Para. 7.   The Tranport will parade at 0830 hours, and will entrain at ROMMERSKIRCHEN at 1000 hours.

Para. 8.   Company stores and blankets will be ready for loading at 0700 hours. The stores of Headquarter Company and Officers' Valises, Mess Kit, &c., will be at the Q.M. Stores at 0530 hours.

DRESS.   Particular attention must be paid to Dress. 2nd Light Brigade instructions T/29 will be strictly adhered to. Mounted Officers will not carry steel helmets.

(Signed)   R.O. BETTS,
Captain & Adjutant,
Queen Victoria's Rifles.

8/7/1919.

A P P E N D I X. III

OUTPOST SECTOR HELD BY 9th LONDON REGIMENT.

Ref. Map 1/25,000 GERMANY
Sheet 2 S.N.W.

The Battalion Sector extends from the RIVER WUPPER (pt. A.58.09) on the Right to RAILWAY BRIDGE at A.0812 on the Left.

The Right Company Sector is the portion of the line from the Brigade boundary, exclusive, to a north and south line through the Cross-roads at A.29.09.

The Left Sector is the portion of the line from the above line, exclusive, to the Battalion Left boundary, inclusive.

Army Form C. 2118.

WAR DIARY or INTELLIGENCE SUMMARY.

9th London Regt Queen Victorias Rifle.

(Erase heading not required.)

Instructions regarding War Diaries and Intelligence Summaries are contained in F. S. Regs., Part II. and the Staff Manual respectively. Title pages will be prepared in manuscript.

Place	Date	Hour	Summary of Events and Information	Remarks and references to Appendices
NAPLD Germany 1/25000 2S SW & NW	1919 Sept 1st		A Coy duties. B Coy Training A-D Coys Outpost line	
	2		" " " " " "	
	3	10.15	Church Parade " " " "	
	4		General Holiday	
	5		A Coy duties B Coy Training A-D Coys Outpost line	
	6		" " " " " "	
	7		" " " " " "	
	8		Examination for 2nd class Army certificate	
	9		" " 3rd " " "	
			act as or of A outpost line. B Coy relieves A Coy on the right. B Coy moving to billets in MALO vacates by B Coy	
	10	10.15	Church Parade	
	11		C Coy duties. D Coy disinfecting clothes billets etc A-B Coy Outpost line	
	12		" D " C " " " "	
	13		" " " " " "	
	14		C Coy Training A-B Coy outpost line	
	15		Bde Sports No parades	

H.R. Day
Lieut: Colonel
O.C. Queen Victorias Rifles

Army Form C. 2118.

WAR DIARY
~~Intelligence~~ of 9th Bn Q.V.R. London Regt Queen Victoria's Rifles
INTELLIGENCE SUMMARY.
(Erase heading not required.)

Instructions regarding War Diaries and Intelligence Summaries are contained in F. S. Regs., Part II. and the Staff Manual respectively. Title pages will be prepared in manuscript.

Place	Date	Hour	Summary of Events and Information	Remarks and references to Appendices
MALO	Aug 17	16.15	To Coy training D Coy duties A+B Coy outpost line	
	18		Church Parade	
	19		C Coy training D "	
	20		" " " "	
	21		" " " " B Coy outpost line A Coy relieved by one Coy 12th R.I. Rifles in the left subsector for boundaries in outpost line now River WUPPER over right to H-S line through Railway Bridge (stations incl.) at A1803 (Germany 1/25000 25 NW)	
	22		A Coy move to billets in MALO	
	23		C Coy training D Coy duties A Coy atthy into billets B Coy outpost line	
			" " " " C Coy relieves B Coy in outpost line B moving	
	24	16.15	to billets vacated by C Coy in MALO	
			Church Parade	
	25		Am (Coo C Coy) Route march To Coy in outpost line	
	26		A"B Coy training B Coy relies C Coy outpost line	
	27		" " " "	

J.R. D ? Lieut: Colonel
O.C. Queen Vic...

Army Form C. 2118.

WAR DIARY
or
Queen Victoria Rifles
INTELLIGENCE SUMMARY.
(Erase heading not required.)

Queen Victoria Regt.

Place	Date	Hour	Summary of Events and Information	Remarks and references to Appendices
MPD	28		A & D Coy training. B Coy duties & Coy outpost line	
	29		"	
	30		"	
	31	10.15	Church Parade.	

J.R. Dann
Lieut: Colonel,
O.C. Queen Victorias Rifles

Headquarters.
2nd Light Brigade.

Herewith War Diary for the month of October.

Captain.
Cmdg: Cadre, 9th Batt: London Regt:
QUEEN VICTORIA'S RIFLES

Army Form C. 2118.

WAR DIARY
or
INTELLIGENCE SUMMARY.
(Erase heading not required.)

Instructions regarding War Diaries and Intelligence Summaries are contained in F. S. Regs., Part II. and the Staff Manual respectively. Title pages will be prepared in manuscript.

Place	Date	Hour	Summary of Events and Information	Remarks and references to Appendices
WALD	1-10-19		1 boy duty. 3 boys training - lecture by M.O. "Venereal"	
"	2-10-19		1 boy firing G.M.C. 1 boy duty - 2 boys training	
"	3-10-19		-do- -do-	
"	4-10-19		-do- -do-	
"	5-10-19	10-15	CHURCH PARADE.	
"	6-10-19		1 boy firing G.M.C. 1 boy duty. 2 boys training	
"	7-10-19		-do- -do-	
"	8-10-19		-do- -do-	
"	9-10-19		-do- -do-	
"	10-10-19		-do- -do-	
"	11-10-19		-do- -do-	
"	12-10-19	10-15	CHURCH PARADE. -do-	
"	13-10-19		1 boy firing G.M.C -do-	
"	14-10-19		-do- -do- A+B Coy amalgamated + to be "No 1 Company"	
"	15-10-19		-do- -do-	
"	16-10-19		D Coy -do- No1 Coy Duty "C" Coy Training - C+D Coy amalgamated + to be No 2 Company	

Army Form C. 2118.

WAR DIARY
or
INTELLIGENCE SUMMARY.
(Erase heading not required.)

Instructions regarding War Diaries and Intelligence Summaries are contained in F. S. Regs., Part II. and the Staff Manual respectively. Title pages will be prepared in manuscript.

Place	Date	Hour	Summary of Events and Information	Remarks and references to Appendices
MALD	17.10.19		No 1 Company duty - ½ No 2 Company firing G.M.C - ½ No 2 Company drawing.	
"	18.10.19		-do-	
"	19.10.19 9.10-15		CHURCH PARADE No 2 Company drawing	
"	20.10.19		No 2 Company duty. No 1 Company drawing	
"	21.10.19		No 1 " " No 2 " "	
"	22.10.19		No 2 " " No 1 " "	
"	23.10.19		No 1 " " No 2 " "	
"	24.10.19		Battalion reduced to Cadre. Returnable men to 13th & 20th Battalions K.R.R.C.	

9th London Regt.
Queen Victoria's Rifles

www.ingramcontent.com/pod-product-compliance
Lightning Source LLC
Chambersburg PA
CBHW081500160426
43193CB00013B/2543